A Kid's Guide to How Vegetables Grow

Patricia Ayers

The Rosen Publishing Group's
PowerKids Press™
New York

Published in 2000 by The Rosen Publishing Group, Inc.
29 East 21st Street, New York, NY 10010

Copyright © 2000 by The Rosen Publishing Group, Inc.

First Edition

Book Design: Maria Melendez

Photo Credits: Cover and title page, pp. 1, 7, 18, 21, 22 © International Stock; pp. 4, 5, 6, 8, 20 © Tony Stone; p. 2, 3, 5, 24 © Super Stock; p. 11, 12, 15, 16 © Corbis-Bettmann.

Ayers, Patricia.
        A kid's guide to how vegetables grow / Patricia Ayers.
            p.   cm. — (Digging in the dirt)
        SUMMARY: Discusses how vegetables grow and describes how to grow your own vegetable garden.
        ISBN 0-8239-5461-7
        1. Vegetable gardening Juvenile literature. 2. Vegetables Juvenile literature. [1. Vegetable gardening. 2. Gardening. 3. Vegetables.] I. Title. II. Series: Ayers, Patricia. Digging in the dirt series.
        SB324 .A96   1999
        635—dc21
                                                                                                99-23632
                                                                                                CIP

Manufactured in the United States of America

Rainbooks 9-K-80 13.75

Contents

All Shapes and Sizes

Vegetables come in all shapes and sizes. When you eat your vegetables, you might be eating the root, the stem, the leaves, the flower, or even the seeds of a plant. Carrots, radishes and beets are really the roots of the plants they grow from. Asparagus spears are plant stems. Potatoes are tubers, or large stems that grow underground. Lettuce and spinach are leaves. Broccoli and cauliflower are flowers. Sweet corn and green peas are seeds, while green beans and snowpeas are pods with seeds inside.

◀ *A vegetable is only a part of the plant it grows from.*

5

Vegetable Magic

Vegetables get their **nutrients** from fertile soil that developed over a long, long time. The nutrients come from **decomposed** plants and animals. Their roots use water to absorb these nutrients. Water carries the nutrients to the plants' leaves. The leaves contain a substance called **chlorophyll**. Chlorophyll helps the plant take in energy from sunlight. The plant uses this energy to turn the water and nutrients into sugar to feed itself. Vegetables also change the nutrients into vitamins and **minerals** your body can use, like iron and calcium. That's why vegetables help you to grow strong bones and teeth and to have healthy blood.

Plants and green vegetables get their color from chlorophyll. ▷

Fruit or Vegetable?

There are a couple of things that help us know whether something is a fruit or a vegetable. According to plant scientists, called botanists, most fruits have seeds while most vegetables don't. Vegetables such as pumpkins, tomatoes, and squash do have seeds, though. However, most people think these are vegetables anyway, because they are **annual** plants, or plants that die each year. Most fruits grow as **perennials**, or plants that live for more than two years. Whatever you want to call them, vegetables are good for you and fun to grow.

◀ *Some scientists say that pumpkins and squash are vegetables, while others say they are fruits.*

9

Choosing Favorites

To grow vegetables, you need only nutrient-rich soil, water, sunlight and seeds. You can grow your favorites in a sunny garden or in pots outside. It is fun to share the work and results with others. The children in Ms. Johnson's science class asked her to help them plan a vegetable garden. First they agreed on what to grow. Since it was early spring, they chose peas because they can be planted in cool weather. They chose beans and lettuce because both can be planted and **harvested** more than once a year. They also decided to grow corn, tomatoes, carrots, squash, and pumpkins. This way they would have harvests from late spring until the fall.

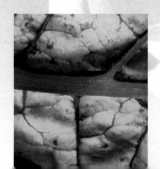

It can be fun to grow your own veggies. ▷

Finding the Right Time

It's important to know when to plant your vegetables. If you plant them when the ground is too cold, the seeds might rot instead of **sprouting**. Also, most vegetables need time to **ripen** before they're picked, so they need to be planted with plenty of time before harvesting.

Most vegetable seeds come in packets that tell you when the seeds should be planted. The directions on the packets also tell you how far apart to plant the seeds and how deep they should go.

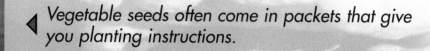
Vegetable seeds often come in packets that give you planting instructions.

Testing the Dirt

Ms. Johnson's class decided how big their garden should be based on the instructions on the seed packets. Then they measured a rectangle that size on the ground, using sticks and strings to outline it. Ms. Johnson explained that digging too early, before the soil is ready, can **compact** the soil and make it harder for plants to grow. She showed the group an **experiment** they could do that would test the soil to see if it was ready. She told them to squeeze a handful of dirt in their hands. If the dirt felt wet and sticky, almost like clay, they would know it wasn't ready. However, the dirt felt dry and crumbly, so the class knew it was time to dig.

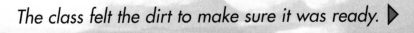

The class felt the dirt to make sure it was ready. ▷

Preparing the Garden

Ms. Johnson's class dug about six inches into the soil, turning over the dirt, breaking it up, and removing all roots, grass, and stones. The children knew their vegetables would be hungry for nutrients. To make sure the soil had enough nutrients to feed the plants, they added **fertilizer** to their garden. Fertilizer can be made from **manure** or from **compost**. You can make your own compost by leaving raw vegetable scraps outside in a pile. Over time, the scraps will **decay**. As they do, they turn into a nutrient-rich mixture that helps plants grow.

◀ *To prepare the soil, the class removed all weeds and stones and mixed in some fertilizer.*

17

Planting Peas

To make the garden bed easy for the seeds to grow in, the class raked it to make it smooth. Because it was still cool outside, they planted the peas first. They placed them in a row at the garden's edge and put up a net that the pea vines could climb as they grew. Pea vines grow upwards, toward the sun, and need something to climb along. This also makes it easier to pick the pea pods, since they're not all jumbled on the ground. The weather was dry, so the class gave the peas plenty of water. This way the water would sink deep into the ground and the plants would have to grow deep roots to reach it. The deeper the roots grow, the stronger the plant will be.

It's important to give your vegetable plants plenty of water. ▷

A Gardening Trick

A few weeks later, as the weather got warmer, the children planted the other seeds. Most vegetables want lots of sun, but lettuce likes some shade, so the students planted the lettuce where taller plants would block the hot summer sun. Ms. Johnson taught her farmers a trick. Carrots are root vegetables, which means that they grow underground. This sometimes makes them hard to find. To help them find the carrots, Ms. Johnson told the class to plant the radishes and carrots in the same row. The fast-growing radish plants marked the line where the tiny carrot leaves would appear.

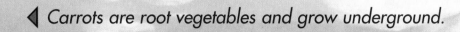

◀ *Carrots are root vegetables and grow underground.*

21

Harvest Time

Different vegetables grow at different speeds. Some, like lettuce and beans, may be full grown in two months. Pumpkins can take four months. They all taste best when they are picked just as they're ripe. The children learned to pick peas and beans leaving the stems on, to pull their carrots carefully from the ground, to cut lettuce from the stems, and to prick a corn kernel to see if it is "milky" before harvesting the ears. They knew the pumpkins were ready when they were big enough to be carved for Halloween. After harvest, the class gathered all the leftover plant parts to make compost to feed next year's garden.

Glossary

annual (AN-yoo-al) Living just one season or one year.

chlorophyll (KLOR-oh-fil) The substance which gives plants their green color and allows them to turn nutrients and energy into sugar.

compact (kom-PAKT) To pack together solidly.

compost (KOM-post) A mixture of decaying vegetable matter, used as fertilizer.

decay (dee-KAY) To rot.

decomposed (dee-kum-POHZD) Decayed or rotted.

experiment (x-SPER-uh-ment) A test to discover something.

fertilizer (FER-tul-y-zer) Material made up of manure, compost, and chemicals added to dirt to make it fertile.

harvest (HAR-vest) To gather in food crops.

manure (ma-NOOR) Animal waste.

minerals (MIN-er-els) Substances occurring in nature.

nutrients (NEW-tree-ents) Things a living thing needs for energy to grow or heal.

perennials (pur-EN-ee-alz) Plants that live two years or more.

ripen (RI-pen) To mature and become ready to eat.

sprouting (SPROUT-ing) Beginning to grow.

23

Index

Web Sites:

To learn more about growing vegetables, check out this Web site:

http://www.urbanext.uiuc.edu/gpe/gpe.html